# The Seasons Journal

MAKK Publishing Co.

San Diego, CA

Copyright © 2024 by Krista Pettiford

All rights reserved. No part of this publication may be reproduced, distributed or transmitted in any form or by any means, including photocopying, recording, or other electronic or mechanical methods, without the prior written permission of the publisher, except in the case of brief quotations embodied in critical reviews and certain other noncommercial uses permitted by copyright law. For permission requests, write to the publisher, addressed "Attention: Permissions Coordinator," at makkpublishing@gmail.com

Unless otherwise indicated Scripture, quotations are from New King James Version®. Copyright © 1982 by Thomas Nelson, Inc. Used by permission. All rights reserved.

Scripture quotations taken from the Amplified® Bible (AMPC), Copyright © 1954, 1958, 1962, 1964, 1965, 1987 by The Lockman Foundation. Used by permission.

This publication is not intended to provide professional advice. It is sold with the understanding that neither the author nor the publisher is engaged in rendering health, medical, or other professional services.

MAKK Publishing Co. San Diego, CA
Kristapettiford.com
Ordering Information:
Quantity sales. Special discounts are available on quantity purchases by corporations, associations, and others. For details, krista4Christ@gmail.com

The Seasons Journal 2024 ISBN: 978-0-9823805-2-9

*Every season has a beginning and an ending, each carrying its own beauty, blessings, purpose, and lessons. As we learn to ask the right questions, we see from Heaven's perspective and begin to recognize God's hand in every stage of our journey.*

— KRISTA PETTIFORD

# WELCOME NOTE

The *Seasons Journal* was created to help you see your season from Heaven's perspective and recognize God's goodness and faithfulness woven into this chapter of your story— so you don't miss out on what He is doing.

Through these pages, you'll be guided to identify your season and gain clarity about what God is calling you to *lean into, listen to, lay down in surrender, keep lifted in prayer*, and *learn*, so you can *make room for* the beauty, blessings, purpose, and lessons He has ordained for you.

Whatever stage or season you find yourself in, my prayer is that this journal will help you be intentional in how you direct your heart, focus on what matters most, and remind you that the Lord is ever mindful of you. May it become a cherished place where you record God's goodness, faithfulness, and the unfolding of His grace and glory in this chapter of your story.

*With grace and gratitude,*
Krista

# CONTENTS

**Identify Your Season**
Discover where you are and what God is doing in this season of your life.

**Five Clarifying Questions for This Season**
Reflect on questions that help you see your circumstances from Heaven's perspective.

**Discover and Record Your Guiding Word for This Season**
Capture the word or phrase God places on your heart as an anchor for this chapter of your story.

**Write Your Vision for This Season**
Write what God is calling you to believe for, build, or become in this season.

**90 Undated Journal Pages**
*Morning* — Begin your day with a declaration and prayer that align your heart with God's purposes.
*Evening* — End your day with gratitude, giving thanks to the Lord for the beauty, blessings, purpose, and lessons He reveals along the way.

**Season Reflections**
At the end of this season, look back with gratitude and reflect on the beauty, blessings, purpose, and lessons God revealed in this season—and what you will carry forward into the next.

The Seasons Journal

# Identify Your Season

**Ecclesiastes 3:1** reminds us that "to everything there is a season, a time for every purpose under heaven." In Hebrew, the word *purpose* means God's desire, delight, or intention. It reveals that every season carries divine meaning—shaped by His love and guided by His will.

**Ecclesiastes 3:11** continues, "He has made everything beautiful in its time." The word *beautiful* comes from the Hebrew *yapheh*, meaning *appropriate, fitting, or made right*. It reminds us that the beauty of a season is not always seen in the moment but unfolds as God brings His purpose to completion. What feels hidden or hard now will reveal its beauty in God's perfect timing.

**SEASONS OF LIFE** can be understood as the times and experiences that mark our journey—periods spent with certain people, in particular places, or walking through unique circumstances that add new chapters to our stories.

**SPIRITUAL SEASONS** mirror the rhythm of nature—winter, spring, summer, and fall. Each carries its own design and divine purpose. Though spiritual seasons don't follow a yearly pattern, they return throughout our lives, bringing opportunities for surrender, growth, and transformation.

**Spring** represents new beginnings—times of planting fresh seeds of faith and sowing what we hope to reap in the future.

**Summer** marks seasons of growth and fruitfulness—when what we've planted begins to bloom and the seeds of God's promises start to prosper in our lives.

**Fall** reflects seasons of harvest—times when we begin to see the full fruit of what we've sown, watered, and waited for with patience and faith.

**Winter** represents pruning seasons—times of darkness, letting go, or waiting when we face trials, tests, and silence from Heaven. Yet even here, the lessons we've learned, the blessings we've gained, the purpose we've discovered, and the beauty we've uncovered in past seasons sustain our hope and give us peace to endure.

When we focus on God's goodness and trust what He is doing, even our winter seasons become sacred times of rest, renewal, and preparation for what's ahead.

Often, the natural seasons of life intertwine with the spiritual seasons of the soul, each one preparing us for what comes next. Every season—no matter how difficult or delightful—has a beginning and an end, each filled with its own beauty, blessings, purpose, and lessons that God has ordained. God uses change—both expected and unexpected—to help us mark our times and recognize the seasons of our lives.

**1 Chronicles 12:32** commends the sons of Issachar, "men who understood the times and knew what Israel should do." In the same way, we are called to discern what God is doing and to see our circumstances from Heaven's perspective—trusting that He is with us, guiding us, and unfolding His purpose in every season of our lives.

**Now it's your turn to pause and reflect.** Take a moment to prayerfully consider where you are right now. What themes, emotions, or patterns are emerging in your life? What has God been speaking, stirring, or shifting within you? As you begin this journal, invite the Holy Spirit to show you the *season you're in*—so you can lean into His work, align with His timing, and embrace the beauty, blessings, purpose, and lessons He is unfolding in this chapter of your story.

The Seasons Journal

## WHAT SEASON ARE YOU IN?

Which of the seasons described above best reflects your current season? Why? Describe what you are experiencing in this time of your life.

# The Seasons Journal

# FIVE CLARIFYING QUESTIONS

On the following pages are five questions to help you see things from Heaven's perspective and clarify God's plan and purpose for your present season.

These questions were birthed in prayer during some of my most difficult seasons. Over time, I've learned to ask them in *every* season—whether difficult or delightful. Each one has helped me shift my perspective, discern God's will, and recognize the beauty, blessings, purpose, and lessons woven throughout each chapter of my story.

As you read and reflect on each question, sit quietly with the Father.

Ask Him to reveal what He wants you to see, teach you what He wants you to learn, and guide you in how to respond to what He is doing in your life right now.

# Lean In

*"But one thing is needed, and Mary has chosen that good portion, which will not be taken away from her."*
— ***Luke 10:42***

To lean in is to focus deeply, giving your full attention to what matters most without allowing distractions to pull you away. It also means focusing what God has called you to do in your current season, whether difficult or delightful, and finding a way to draw strength, wisdom, and blessing from it through faith, courage, and perseverance.

We are always called to lean into God's presence and His Word, to fellowship with Him and continue growing spiritually. Yet, within each season, God reveals something specific—a principle to live by, a purpose to pursue, a promise to hold onto, or a plan to walk out—that He invites you to lean into.

Ask the Father to show you the one—or few—things He wants you to lean into right now. He may surprise you. It may be something that has never even occurred to you. Once He reveals it, fix your focus there. Whether or not you fully understand His reasons, your obedience will open the way for Him to reveal what He has already prepared for you.

**PRAYER:** *Father, please show me the one or few things you would have me lean into during this season.*

The Seasons Journal

## WRITE WHAT HE SHOWS YOU

# LISTEN

*"My sheep hear My voice; I know them, and they follow Me."*
— **John 10:27**

The Greek word translated *hear* in John 10:27 is *akouō*, which means to listen attentively, understand, and respond. Listening goes beyond the simple act of hearing sound—it involves giving thoughtful attention with the intent to comprehend and act upon what is heard. When it comes to God's voice, we are called not only to hear but to *listen*—to understand His heart and obey what He speaks.

In every season, many voices will compete for your attention—but not every voice will come from God. His voice, and the voices He uses to speak to you, will always align with His Word and His will. God's voice brings clarity, peace, and direction. It corrects in love, instructs with wisdom, and guides you in truth.

Ask the Father to teach you how to discern His voice from the voices around you that would lead you astray. Ask Him to help you learn to know His voice and obey when He speaks by His written Word, by His Spirit, and through the people He places in your life.

**PRAYER:** *Father, help me discern Your voice from every other voice. Teach me to recognize when doubt, fear, or negativity try to speak into my life, and give me the courage to silence them. Stir a hunger in me for Your Word and open my ears to hear Your truth. Help me recognize and respond to the voices of wisdom, counsel, and guidance You send to encourage and equip me in this season.*

The Seasons Journal

## WRITE WHAT YOU HEAR

# Lay Down

*"Unless a kernel of wheat falls to the ground and dies, it remains alone; but if it dies, it produces much fruit."*
— **John 12:24**

To lay something down is to surrender your hold on it and entrust it to God—allowing Him to do whatever He desires with it.

In every season, there will be things God asks you to lay down. Sometimes, He calls you to release something temporarily; other times, He asks for a complete surrender. Either way, obedience opens the way for Him to bring forth something new.

Abraham's story in Genesis 22 shows us this truth. God asked him to lay down Isaac—the son of promise. Abraham obeyed, trusting that even if the promise had to die, God could raise it again it that was His will. In the same way, when we lay down what God asks of us, we totally surrender it to His will, and make room for His greater purpose to unfold.

Surrender isn't easy, especially when what we're asked to release is precious to us. But every act of obedience becomes a seed of faith—planted in trust and destined to bear fruit in God's perfect timing.

**PRAYER:** *Father, what would You have me lay down in this season? Give me the grace to surrender it fully into Your hands and the faith to trust that Your plans for me are good.*

The Seasons Journal

## WRITE WHAT HE SHOWS YOU

# LIFT IN PRAYER

*"Then He took the five loaves and the two fish, and looking up to heaven, He blessed and broke them, and gave them to the disciples to set before the multitude."*
— **Luke 9:16**

In the same way Jesus looked up to heaven, blessed the bread and fish, and multiplied them to feed the multitude, prayer is an act of lifting something or someone—up to the Lord. When you lift matters to Him in faith, you invite His blessing over what you bring and trust that He can do exceedingly and abundantly above all you could ask, think, or imagine.

Just as God sometimes asks you to lay things down, there are also people, plans, and purposes He instructs you to keep lifted before Him in prayer. These are the ones He has entrusted to your spiritual care—to bless, heal, restore, redeem, and multiply through your faith-filled intercession.

Find faithful prayer partners who will stand with you and agree in prayer for what God has placed on your heart. Together, commit to continue lifting those people, situations, and dreams before Him until you see breakthrough and blessing unfold.

**PRAYER:** *Father, who and what would You have me keep lifted before You in prayer this season? Give me the endurance to prayer without ceasing and surround me with prayer partners who will agree with me in faith as we lift Your purposes together before Heaven.*

The Seasons Journal

## WRITE WHAT HE SHOWS YOU

# LEARN

*"I will instruct you and teach you in the way you should go; I will counsel you with My loving eye on you."*
— **Psalm 32:8**

Every season carries lessons to be learned. Often, the most challenging seasons produce the most transformative lessons—but even in delightful seasons, there is wisdom waiting to be discovered.

In times of ease, the lessons God wants you to learn are sometimes the hardest to discern. Yet those very lessons will sustain you through seasons of drought, silence, testing, and trials.

Choose to remain teachable and willing to learn in every season, and God will give you understanding. He will reveal the lessons He has ordained for you, shaping your heart through His instruction, direction, correction, and grace.

Look for the lessons life offers you daily. Be willing to unlearn what is no longer fruitful and open your heart to learn new ways that lead to growth and transformation.

**PRAYER:** *Father, give me understanding and a teachable spirit. Help me discern the one—or few—things You would have me learn in this season. Grant me wisdom to recognize what to release and grace to receive the lessons You are teaching me.*

The Seasons Journal

## **WRITE WHAT HE SHOWS YOU**

# WRITE YOUR VISION

*"Write the vision; make it plain on tablets, so she may run who reads it. For still the vision awaits its appointed time, it hastens its end— it will not lie. If it seems slow, wait for it; it will sure come."*
— **Habakkuk 2:2**

Ask God to give you *one cohesive vision* of what He is leading you toward in what God is calling you to *lean into, listen to, lay down, keep lifted in prayer*, and *learn* during this season. Write then vision and let it become your spiritual compass—a reminder of where God is leading you and how He is shaping your heart through each of assignment. As you write, invite the Holy Spirit to give you wisdom, clarity, and courage to pursue what He shows you.

**Prayer:** *Father, give me one cohesive vision for this season—eyes to see what You are revealing, faith to follow where You are leading, and grace to run my race.*

_____
_____
_____
_____
_____
_____
_____
_____
_____
_____

# The Seasons Journal

# Your Guiding Word

*"Your word is a lamp to my feet and a light to my path."*
— **Psalm 119:105**

Think of *your word* as a *motto*—one word or a simple statement that captures your guiding belief for this season. A motto reflects a core value, belief, or principle. When consistently lived out, it reinforces your faith and helps you stay focused on what God has called you to do.

To discover your word or create your motto for the season, ask God to reveal the *principle* or *core value* that will help you stay focused and faithful in this season.

Look for a scripture that embodies the values, principles, or beliefs you want to guide your heart and actions right now. If you don't have a specific verse, write down a word, phrase, or declaration that expresses what you believe God is forming in you during this season.

**PRAYER:** *Father, let the word You give me for this season shape my world. May what I think, speak, and do align with Your truth. Let this word—birthed in Your presence—anchor my heart, guide my steps, and remind me that Your light leads me forward in every season.*

**Write your word or motto for this season.**

_____

_____

_____

# Journaling Pages

*Give thanks
for the beauty, blessings, purpose,
and lessons each day brings.*

## Journal Pages Include:

**Morning**
Begin your day with a declaration to help you stay focused on what God has called you to do in this season. Followed with a prayer to recognize and *capture* the beauty, blessings, purpose, and lessons the day holds for you.

**Evening**
End your day with gratitude—a space to give thanks to the Lord and *capture* the beauty, blessings, purpose, and lessons He revealed throughout your day.

## BEAUTY BLESSING PURPOSE LESSONS

Each day holds beauty, blessings, purpose, and lessons waiting to be discovered. Take a moment to pause, reflect, and recognize God's hand in each one.

### Beauty
*"He has made everything beautiful in its time."*
— Ecclesiastes 3:11
*Lord, help me see the beauty You are revealing in this season.*

### Blessings
*"For You meet him with the blessings of goodness; You set a crown of pure gold upon his head."*
— Psalm 21:3
*Father, thank You for the blessings of goodness You've already placed before me.*

### Purpose
*"And we know that all things work together for good to those who love God, to those who are the called according to His purpose."*
— Romans 8:28
*God, remind me that everything in my life is working together for Your purpose.*

### Lessons
*"He awakens Me morning by morning, He awakens My ear to hear as the learned."*
— Isaiah 50:4
*Lord, awaken my heart each day to hear and learn from You.*

The Seasons Journal

**Date:** _____

### Morning Declaration & Prayer
Today, I will *lean into* the things God has called me to give my heart and focus to.
I will *listen and obey* God's voice.
I will *trust His plan* and *lay down* the things I'm not called to carry in this season.
I will *lift in prayer* the people, situations, and dreams God has entrusted to me.
I will remain *teachable* and embrace the lessons today brings.

**Prayer:** Father, open my eyes and heart to perceive things from Heaven's perspective and to recognize the beauty, blessings, purpose, and lessons this day holds.

### Evening Gratitude
Father, thank You for the beauty, blessings, purpose, and lessons You revealed today.

_____

_____

_____

_____

_____

_____

_____

_____

_____

The Seasons Journal

**Date:** _____

### Morning Declaration & Prayer

Today, I will *lean into* the things God has called me to give my heart and focus to.
I will *listen and obey* God's voice.
I will *trust His plan* and *lay down* the things I'm not called to carry in this season.
I will *lift in prayer* the people, situations, and dreams God has entrusted to me.
I will remain *teachable* and embrace the lessons today brings.

**Prayer:** Father, open my eyes and heart to perceive things from Heaven's perspective and to recognize the beauty, blessings, purpose, and lessons this day holds.

### Evening Gratitude

Father, thank You for the beauty, blessings, purpose, and lessons You revealed today.

_____

_____

_____

_____

_____

_____

_____

_____

_____

The Seasons Journal

**Date:** _____

### Morning Declaration & Prayer
Today, I will *lean into* the things God has called me to give my heart and focus to.
I will *listen and obey* God's voice.
I will *trust His plan* and *lay down* the things I'm not called to carry in this season.
I will *lift in prayer* the people, situations, and dreams God has entrusted to me.
I will remain *teachable* and embrace the lessons today brings.

**Prayer:** Father, open my eyes and heart to perceive things from Heaven's perspective and to recognize the beauty, blessings, purpose, and lessons this day holds.

### Evening Gratitude
Father, thank You for the beauty, blessings, purpose, and lessons You revealed today.

_____

_____

_____

_____

_____

_____

_____

_____

The Seasons Journal

**Date:** _____

### Morning Declaration & Prayer
Today, I will *lean into* the things God has called me to give my heart and focus to.
I will *listen and obey* God's voice.
I will *trust His plan* and *lay down* the things I'm not called to carry in this season.
I will *lift in prayer* the people, situations, and dreams God has entrusted to me.
I will remain *teachable* and embrace the lessons today brings.

**Prayer:** Father, open my eyes and heart to perceive things from Heaven's perspective and to recognize the beauty, blessings, purpose, and lessons this day holds.

### Evening Gratitude
Father, thank You for the beauty, blessings, purpose, and lessons You revealed today.

_____

_____

_____

_____

_____

_____

_____

_____

The Seasons Journal

**Date:** _____

### Morning Declaration & Prayer

Today, I will *lean into* the things God has called me to give my heart and focus to.
I will *listen and obey* God's voice.
I will *trust His plan* and *lay down* the things I'm not called to carry in this season.
I will *lift in prayer* the people, situations, and dreams God has entrusted to me.
I will remain *teachable* and embrace the lessons today brings.

**Prayer:** Father, open my eyes and heart to perceive things from Heaven's perspective and to recognize the beauty, blessings, purpose, and lessons this day holds.

### Evening Gratitude

Father, thank You for the beauty, blessings, purpose, and lessons You revealed today.

_____

_____

_____

_____

_____

_____

_____

_____

_____

The Seasons Journal

**Date:** _____

### Morning Declaration & Prayer

Today, I will *lean into* the things God has called me to give my heart and focus to.
I will *listen and obey* God's voice.
I will *trust His plan* and *lay down* the things I'm not called to carry in this season.
I will *lift in prayer* the people, situations, and dreams God has entrusted to me.
I will remain *teachable* and embrace the lessons today brings.

**Prayer:** Father, open my eyes and heart to perceive things from Heaven's perspective and to recognize the beauty, blessings, purpose, and lessons this day holds.

### Evening Gratitude

Father, thank You for the beauty, blessings, purpose, and lessons You revealed today.

_____

_____

_____

_____

_____

_____

_____

_____

The Seasons Journal

**Date:** _____


### Morning Declaration & Prayer

Today, I will *lean into* the things God has called me to give my heart and focus to.

I will *listen and obey* God's voice.

I will *trust His plan* and *lay down* the things I'm not called to carry in this season.

I will *lift in prayer* the people, situations, and dreams God has entrusted to me.

I will remain *teachable* and embrace the lessons today brings.


**Prayer:** Father, open my eyes and heart to perceive things from Heaven's perspective and to recognize the beauty, blessings, purpose, and lessons this day holds.


### Evening Gratitude

Father, thank You for the beauty, blessings, purpose, and lessons You revealed today.

_____

_____

_____

_____

_____

_____

_____

_____

_____

The Seasons Journal

**Date:** _____

### Morning Declaration & Prayer

Today, I will *lean into* the things God has called me to give my heart and focus to.
I will *listen and obey* God's voice.
I will *trust His plan* and *lay down* the things I'm not called to carry in this season.
I will *lift in prayer* the people, situations, and dreams God has entrusted to me.
I will remain *teachable* and embrace the lessons today brings.

**Prayer:** Father, open my eyes and heart to perceive things from Heaven's perspective and to recognize the beauty, blessings, purpose, and lessons this day holds.

### Evening Gratitude

Father, thank You for the beauty, blessings, purpose, and lessons You revealed today.

_____

_____

_____

_____

_____

_____

_____

_____

The Seasons Journal

**Date:** _____

### Morning Declaration & Prayer

Today, I will *lean into* the things God has called me to give my heart and focus to.
I will *listen and obey* God's voice.
I will *trust His plan* and *lay down* the things I'm not called to carry in this season.
I will *lift in prayer* the people, situations, and dreams God has entrusted to me.
I will remain *teachable* and embrace the lessons today brings.

**Prayer:** Father, open my eyes and heart to perceive things from Heaven's perspective and to recognize the beauty, blessings, purpose, and lessons this day holds.

### Evening Gratitude

Father, thank You for the beauty, blessings, purpose, and lessons You revealed today.

_____

_____

_____

_____

_____

_____

_____

_____

_____

The Seasons Journal

**Date:** _____

### Morning Declaration & Prayer
Today, I will *lean into* the things God has called me to give my heart and focus to.
I will *listen and obey* God's voice.
I will *trust His plan* and *lay down* the things I'm not called to carry in this season.
I will *lift in prayer* the people, situations, and dreams God has entrusted to me.
I will remain *teachable* and embrace the lessons today brings.

**Prayer:** Father, open my eyes and heart to perceive things from Heaven's perspective and to recognize the beauty, blessings, purpose, and lessons this day holds.

### Evening Gratitude
Father, thank You for the beauty, blessings, purpose, and lessons You revealed today.

_____

_____

_____

_____

_____

_____

_____

_____

The Seasons Journal

**Date:** _____

### Morning Declaration & Prayer

Today, I will *lean into* the things God has called me to give my heart and focus to.
I will *listen and obey* God's voice.
I will *trust His plan* and *lay down* the things I'm not called to carry in this season.
I will *lift in prayer* the people, situations, and dreams God has entrusted to me.
I will remain *teachable* and embrace the lessons today brings.

**Prayer:** Father, open my eyes and heart to perceive things from Heaven's perspective and to recognize the beauty, blessings, purpose, and lessons this day holds.

### Evening Gratitude

Father, thank You for the beauty, blessings, purpose, and lessons You revealed today.

_____

_____

_____

_____

_____

_____

_____

_____

The Seasons Journal

**Date:** _____

### Morning Declaration & Prayer

Today, I will *lean into* the things God has called me to give my heart and focus to.
I will *listen and obey* God's voice.
I will *trust His plan* and *lay down* the things I'm not called to carry in this season.
I will *lift in prayer* the people, situations, and dreams God has entrusted to me.
I will remain *teachable* and embrace the lessons today brings.

**Prayer:** Father, open my eyes and heart to perceive things from Heaven's perspective and to recognize the beauty, blessings, purpose, and lessons this day holds.

### Evening Gratitude

Father, thank You for the beauty, blessings, purpose, and lessons You revealed today.

_____

_____

_____

_____

_____

_____

_____

_____

The Seasons Journal

**Date:** _____

### Morning Declaration & Prayer

Today, I will *lean into* the things God has called me to give my heart and focus to.
I will *listen and obey* God's voice.
I will *trust His plan* and *lay down* the things I'm not called to carry in this season.
I will *lift in prayer* the people, situations, and dreams God has entrusted to me.
I will remain *teachable* and embrace the lessons today brings.

**Prayer:** Father, open my eyes and heart to perceive things from Heaven's perspective and to recognize the beauty, blessings, purpose, and lessons this day holds.

### Evening Gratitude

Father, thank You for the beauty, blessings, purpose, and lessons You revealed today.

_____

_____

_____

_____

_____

_____

_____

_____

_____

The Seasons Journal

**Date:** _____

### Morning Declaration & Prayer

Today, I will *lean into* the things God has called me to give my heart and focus to.
I will *listen and obey* God's voice.
I will *trust His plan* and *lay down* the things I'm not called to carry in this season.
I will *lift in prayer* the people, situations, and dreams God has entrusted to me.
I will remain *teachable* and embrace the lessons today brings.

**Prayer:** Father, open my eyes and heart to perceive things from Heaven's perspective and to recognize the beauty, blessings, purpose, and lessons this day holds.

### Evening Gratitude

Father, thank You for the beauty, blessings, purpose, and lessons You revealed today.

_____

_____

_____

_____

_____

_____

_____

_____

The Seasons Journal

**Date:** _____

## Morning Declaration & Prayer

Today, I will *lean into* the things God has called me to give my heart and focus to.
I will *listen and obey* God's voice.
I will *trust His plan* and *lay down* the things I'm not called to carry in this season.
I will *lift in prayer* the people, situations, and dreams God has entrusted to me.
I will remain *teachable* and embrace the lessons today brings.

**Prayer:** Father, open my eyes and heart to perceive things from Heaven's perspective and to recognize the beauty, blessings, purpose, and lessons this day holds.

## Evening Gratitude

Father, thank You for the beauty, blessings, purpose, and lessons You revealed today.

_____

_____

_____

_____

_____

_____

_____

_____

The Seasons Journal

**Date:** _____

### Morning Declaration & Prayer
Today, I will *lean into* the things God has called me to give my heart and focus to.
I will *listen and obey* God's voice.
I will *trust His plan* and *lay down* the things I'm not called to carry in this season.
I will *lift in prayer* the people, situations, and dreams God has entrusted to me.
I will remain *teachable* and embrace the lessons today brings.

**Prayer:** Father, open my eyes and heart to perceive things from Heaven's perspective and to recognize the beauty, blessings, purpose, and lessons this day holds.

### Evening Gratitude
Father, thank You for the beauty, blessings, purpose, and lessons You revealed today.

_____

_____

_____

_____

_____

_____

_____

_____

_____

The Seasons Journal

**Date:** _____

### Morning Declaration & Prayer

Today, I will *lean into* the things God has called me to give my heart and focus to.
I will *listen and obey* God's voice.
I will *trust His plan* and *lay down* the things I'm not called to carry in this season.
I will *lift in prayer* the people, situations, and dreams God has entrusted to me.
I will remain *teachable* and embrace the lessons today brings.

**Prayer:** Father, open my eyes and heart to perceive things from Heaven's perspective and to recognize the beauty, blessings, purpose, and lessons this day holds.

### Evening Gratitude

Father, thank You for the beauty, blessings, purpose, and lessons You revealed today.

_____

_____

_____

_____

_____

_____

_____

_____

The Seasons Journal

**Date:** _____

### Morning Declaration & Prayer
Today, I will *lean into* the things God has called me to give my heart and focus to.
I will *listen and obey* God's voice.
I will *trust His plan* and *lay down* the things I'm not called to carry in this season.
I will *lift in prayer* the people, situations, and dreams God has entrusted to me.
I will remain *teachable* and embrace the lessons today brings.

**Prayer:** Father, open my eyes and heart to perceive things from Heaven's perspective and to recognize the beauty, blessings, purpose, and lessons this day holds.

### Evening Gratitude
Father, thank You for the beauty, blessings, purpose, and lessons You revealed today.

_____

_____

_____

_____

_____

_____

_____

_____

The Seasons Journal

**Date:** _____

## Morning Declaration & Prayer

Today, I will *lean into* the things God has called me to give my heart and focus to.
I will *listen and obey* God's voice.
I will *trust His plan* and *lay down* the things I'm not called to carry in this season.
I will *lift in prayer* the people, situations, and dreams God has entrusted to me.
I will remain *teachable* and embrace the lessons today brings.

**Prayer:** Father, open my eyes and heart to perceive things from Heaven's perspective and to recognize the beauty, blessings, purpose, and lessons this day holds.

## Evening Gratitude

Father, thank You for the beauty, blessings, purpose, and lessons You revealed today.

_____

_____

_____

_____

_____

_____

_____

_____

_____

The Seasons Journal

**Date:** _____

### Morning Declaration & Prayer

Today, I will *lean into* the things God has called me to give my heart and focus to.
I will *listen and obey* God's voice.
I will *trust His plan* and *lay down* the things I'm not called to carry in this season.
I will *lift in prayer* the people, situations, and dreams God has entrusted to me.
I will remain *teachable* and embrace the lessons today brings.

**Prayer:** Father, open my eyes and heart to perceive things from Heaven's perspective and to recognize the beauty, blessings, purpose, and lessons this day holds.

### Evening Gratitude

Father, thank You for the beauty, blessings, purpose, and lessons You revealed today.

_____

_____

_____

_____

_____

_____

_____

_____

The Seasons Journal

**Date:** _____

### Morning Declaration & Prayer
Today, I will *lean into* the things God has called me to give my heart and focus to.
I will *listen and obey* God's voice.
I will *trust His plan* and *lay down* the things I'm not called to carry in this season.
I will *lift in prayer* the people, situations, and dreams God has entrusted to me.
I will remain *teachable* and embrace the lessons today brings.

**Prayer:** Father, open my eyes and heart to perceive things from Heaven's perspective and to recognize the beauty, blessings, purpose, and lessons this day holds.

### Evening Gratitude
Father, thank You for the beauty, blessings, purpose, and lessons You revealed today.

_____

_____

_____

_____

_____

_____

_____

_____

_____

The Seasons Journal

**Date:** _____

### Morning Declaration & Prayer

Today, I will *lean into* the things God has called me to give my heart and focus to.
I will *listen and obey* God's voice.
I will *trust His plan* and *lay down* the things I'm not called to carry in this season.
I will *lift in prayer* the people, situations, and dreams God has entrusted to me.
I will remain *teachable* and embrace the lessons today brings.

**Prayer:** Father, open my eyes and heart to perceive things from Heaven's perspective and to recognize the beauty, blessings, purpose, and lessons this day holds.

### Evening Gratitude

Father, thank You for the beauty, blessings, purpose, and lessons You revealed today.

_____

_____

_____

_____

_____

_____

_____

_____

The Seasons Journal

**Date:** _____

### Morning Declaration & Prayer

Today, I will *lean into* the things God has called me to give my heart and focus to.
I will *listen and obey* God's voice.
I will *trust His plan* and *lay down* the things I'm not called to carry in this season.
I will *lift in prayer* the people, situations, and dreams God has entrusted to me.
I will remain *teachable* and embrace the lessons today brings.

**Prayer:** Father, open my eyes and heart to perceive things from Heaven's perspective and to recognize the beauty, blessings, purpose, and lessons this day holds.

### Evening Gratitude

Father, thank You for the beauty, blessings, purpose, and lessons You revealed today.

_____

_____

_____

_____

_____

_____

_____

_____

The Seasons Journal

**Date:** _____

### Morning Declaration & Prayer

Today, I will *lean into* the things God has called me to give my heart and focus to.
I will *listen and obey* God's voice.
I will *trust His plan* and *lay down* the things I'm not called to carry in this season.
I will *lift in prayer* the people, situations, and dreams God has entrusted to me.
I will remain *teachable* and embrace the lessons today brings.

**Prayer:** Father, open my eyes and heart to perceive things from Heaven's perspective and to recognize the beauty, blessings, purpose, and lessons this day holds.

### Evening Gratitude

Father, thank You for the beauty, blessings, purpose, and lessons You revealed today.

_____

_____

_____

_____

_____

_____

_____

_____

The Seasons Journal

**Date:** _____

## Morning Declaration & Prayer

Today, I will *lean into* the things God has called me to give my heart and focus to.
I will *listen and obey* God's voice.
I will *trust His plan* and *lay down* the things I'm not called to carry in this season.
I will *lift in prayer* the people, situations, and dreams God has entrusted to me.
I will remain *teachable* and embrace the lessons today brings.

**Prayer:** Father, open my eyes and heart to perceive things from Heaven's perspective and to recognize the beauty, blessings, purpose, and lessons this day holds.

## Evening Gratitude

Father, thank You for the beauty, blessings, purpose, and lessons You revealed today.

_____

_____

_____

_____

_____

_____

_____

_____

_____

The Seasons Journal

**Date:** _____

### Morning Declaration & Prayer

Today, I will *lean into* the things God has called me to give my heart and focus to.
I will *listen and obey* God's voice.
I will *trust His plan* and *lay down* the things I'm not called to carry in this season.
I will *lift in prayer* the people, situations, and dreams God has entrusted to me.
I will remain *teachable* and embrace the lessons today brings.

**Prayer:** Father, open my eyes and heart to perceive things from Heaven's perspective and to recognize the beauty, blessings, purpose, and lessons this day holds.

### Evening Gratitude

Father, thank You for the beauty, blessings, purpose, and lessons You revealed today.

_____

_____

_____

_____

_____

_____

_____

_____

The Seasons Journal

**Date:** _____

## Morning Declaration & Prayer

Today, I will *lean into* the things God has called me to give my heart and focus to.
I will *listen and obey* God's voice.
I will *trust His plan* and *lay down* the things I'm not called to carry in this season.
I will *lift in prayer* the people, situations, and dreams God has entrusted to me.
I will remain *teachable* and embrace the lessons today brings.

**Prayer:** Father, open my eyes and heart to perceive things from Heaven's perspective and to recognize the beauty, blessings, purpose, and lessons this day holds.

## Evening Gratitude

Father, thank You for the beauty, blessings, purpose, and lessons You revealed today.

_____

_____

_____

_____

_____

_____

_____

_____

_____

The Seasons Journal

**Date:** _____

### Morning Declaration & Prayer

Today, I will *lean into* the things God has called me to give my heart and focus to.
I will *listen and obey* God's voice.
I will *trust His plan* and *lay down* the things I'm not called to carry in this season.
I will *lift in prayer* the people, situations, and dreams God has entrusted to me.
I will remain *teachable* and embrace the lessons today brings.

**Prayer:** Father, open my eyes and heart to perceive things from Heaven's perspective and to recognize the beauty, blessings, purpose, and lessons this day holds.

### Evening Gratitude

Father, thank You for the beauty, blessings, purpose, and lessons You revealed today.

_____

_____

_____

_____

_____

_____

_____

_____

The Seasons Journal

**Date:** _____

### Morning Declaration & Prayer

Today, I will *lean into* the things God has called me to give my heart and focus to.
I will *listen and obey* God's voice.
I will *trust His plan* and *lay down* the things I'm not called to carry in this season.
I will *lift in prayer* the people, situations, and dreams God has entrusted to me.
I will remain *teachable* and embrace the lessons today brings.

**Prayer:** Father, open my eyes and heart to perceive things from Heaven's perspective and to recognize the beauty, blessings, purpose, and lessons this day holds.

### Evening Gratitude

Father, thank You for the beauty, blessings, purpose, and lessons You revealed today.

_____

_____

_____

_____

_____

_____

_____

_____

The Seasons Journal

**Date:** _____

### Morning Declaration & Prayer

Today, I will *lean into* the things God has called me to give my heart and focus to.

I will *listen and obey* God's voice.

I will *trust His plan* and *lay down* the things I'm not called to carry in this season.

I will *lift in prayer* the people, situations, and dreams God has entrusted to me.

I will remain *teachable* and embrace the lessons today brings.

**Prayer:** Father, open my eyes and heart to perceive things from Heaven's perspective and to recognize the beauty, blessings, purpose, and lessons this day holds.

### Evening Gratitude

Father, thank You for the beauty, blessings, purpose, and lessons You revealed today.

_____

_____

_____

_____

_____

_____

_____

The Seasons Journal

**Date:** _____

### Morning Declaration & Prayer

Today, I will *lean into* the things God has called me to give my heart and focus to.
I will *listen and obey* God's voice.
I will *trust His plan* and *lay down* the things I'm not called to carry in this season.
I will *lift in prayer* the people, situations, and dreams God has entrusted to me.
I will remain *teachable* and embrace the lessons today brings.

**Prayer:** Father, open my eyes and heart to perceive things from Heaven's perspective and to recognize the beauty, blessings, purpose, and lessons this day holds.

### Evening Gratitude

Father, thank You for the beauty, blessings, purpose, and lessons You revealed today.

_____

_____

_____

_____

_____

_____

_____

_____

The Seasons Journal

**Date:** _____

### Morning Declaration & Prayer

Today, I will *lean into* the things God has called me to give my heart and focus to.
I will *listen and obey* God's voice.
I will *trust His plan* and *lay down* the things I'm not called to carry in this season.
I will *lift in prayer* the people, situations, and dreams God has entrusted to me.
I will remain *teachable* and embrace the lessons today brings.

**Prayer:** Father, open my eyes and heart to perceive things from Heaven's perspective and to recognize the beauty, blessings, purpose, and lessons this day holds.

### Evening Gratitude

Father, thank You for the beauty, blessings, purpose, and lessons You revealed today.

_____

_____

_____

_____

_____

_____

_____

_____

The Seasons Journal

**Date:** _____

## Morning Declaration & Prayer

Today, I will *lean into* the things God has called me to give my heart and focus to.
I will *listen and obey* God's voice.
I will *trust His plan* and *lay down* the things I'm not called to carry in this season.
I will *lift in prayer* the people, situations, and dreams God has entrusted to me.
I will remain *teachable* and embrace the lessons today brings.

**Prayer:** Father, open my eyes and heart to perceive things from Heaven's perspective and to recognize the beauty, blessings, purpose, and lessons this day holds.

## Evening Gratitude

Father, thank You for the beauty, blessings, purpose, and lessons You revealed today.

_____

_____

_____

_____

_____

_____

_____

_____

The Seasons Journal

**Date:** _____

### Morning Declaration & Prayer
Today, I will *lean into* the things God has called me to give my heart and focus to.
I will *listen and obey* God's voice.
I will *trust His plan* and *lay down* the things I'm not called to carry in this season.
I will *lift in prayer* the people, situations, and dreams God has entrusted to me.
I will remain *teachable* and embrace the lessons today brings.

**Prayer:** Father, open my eyes and heart to perceive things from Heaven's perspective and to recognize the beauty, blessings, purpose, and lessons this day holds.

### Evening Gratitude
Father, thank You for the beauty, blessings, purpose, and lessons You revealed today.

_____

_____

_____

_____

_____

_____

_____

_____

The Seasons Journal

**Date:** _____

### Morning Declaration & Prayer

Today, I will *lean into* the things God has called me to give my heart and focus to.
I will *listen and obey* God's voice.
I will *trust His plan* and *lay down* the things I'm not called to carry in this season.
I will *lift in prayer* the people, situations, and dreams God has entrusted to me.
I will remain *teachable* and embrace the lessons today brings.

**Prayer:** Father, open my eyes and heart to perceive things from Heaven's perspective and to recognize the beauty, blessings, purpose, and lessons this day holds.

### Evening Gratitude

Father, thank You for the beauty, blessings, purpose, and lessons You revealed today.

_____

_____

_____

_____

_____

_____

_____

_____

The Seasons Journal

**Date:** _____

### Morning Declaration & Prayer

Today, I will *lean into* the things God has called me to give my heart and focus to.
I will *listen and obey* God's voice.
I will *trust His plan* and *lay down* the things I'm not called to carry in this season.
I will *lift in prayer* the people, situations, and dreams God has entrusted to me.
I will remain *teachable* and embrace the lessons today brings.

**Prayer:** Father, open my eyes and heart to perceive things from Heaven's perspective and to recognize the beauty, blessings, purpose, and lessons this day holds.

### Evening Gratitude

Father, thank You for the beauty, blessings, purpose, and lessons You revealed today.

_____

_____

_____

_____

_____

_____

_____

The Seasons Journal

**Date:** _____

### Morning Declaration & Prayer

Today, I will *lean into* the things God has called me to give my heart and focus to.
I will *listen and obey* God's voice.
I will *trust His plan* and *lay down* the things I'm not called to carry in this season.
I will *lift in prayer* the people, situations, and dreams God has entrusted to me.
I will remain *teachable* and embrace the lessons today brings.

**Prayer:** Father, open my eyes and heart to perceive things from Heaven's perspective and to recognize the beauty, blessings, purpose, and lessons this day holds.

### Evening Gratitude

Father, thank You for the beauty, blessings, purpose, and lessons You revealed today.

_____

_____

_____

_____

_____

_____

_____

_____

_____

The Seasons Journal

**Date:** _____

### Morning Declaration & Prayer

Today, I will *lean into* the things God has called me to give my heart and focus to.
I will *listen and obey* God's voice.
I will *trust His plan* and *lay down* the things I'm not called to carry in this season.
I will *lift in prayer* the people, situations, and dreams God has entrusted to me.
I will remain *teachable* and embrace the lessons today brings.

**Prayer:** Father, open my eyes and heart to perceive things from Heaven's perspective and to recognize the beauty, blessings, purpose, and lessons this day holds.

### Evening Gratitude

Father, thank You for the beauty, blessings, purpose, and lessons You revealed today.

_____

_____

_____

_____

_____

_____

_____

_____

The Seasons Journal

**Date:** _____

## Morning Declaration & Prayer

Today, I will *lean into* the things God has called me to give my heart and focus to.
I will *listen and obey* God's voice.
I will *trust His plan* and *lay down* the things I'm not called to carry in this season.
I will *lift in prayer* the people, situations, and dreams God has entrusted to me.
I will remain *teachable* and embrace the lessons today brings.

**Prayer:** Father, open my eyes and heart to perceive things from Heaven's perspective and to recognize the beauty, blessings, purpose, and lessons this day holds.

## Evening Gratitude

Father, thank You for the beauty, blessings, purpose, and lessons You revealed today.

_____

_____

_____

_____

_____

_____

_____

_____

The Seasons Journal

**Date:** _____

### Morning Declaration & Prayer

Today, I will *lean into* the things God has called me to give my heart and focus to.
I will *listen and obey* God's voice.
I will *trust His plan* and *lay down* the things I'm not called to carry in this season.
I will *lift in prayer* the people, situations, and dreams God has entrusted to me.
I will remain *teachable* and embrace the lessons today brings.

**Prayer:** Father, open my eyes and heart to perceive things from Heaven's perspective and to recognize the beauty, blessings, purpose, and lessons this day holds.

### Evening Gratitude

Father, thank You for the beauty, blessings, purpose, and lessons You revealed today.

_____

_____

_____

_____

_____

_____

_____

_____

The Seasons Journal

**Date:** _____

## Morning Declaration & Prayer

Today, I will *lean into* the things God has called me to give my heart and focus to.
I will *listen and obey* God's voice.
I will *trust His plan* and *lay down* the things I'm not called to carry in this season.
I will *lift in prayer* the people, situations, and dreams God has entrusted to me.
I will remain *teachable* and embrace the lessons today brings.

**Prayer:** Father, open my eyes and heart to perceive things from Heaven's perspective and to recognize the beauty, blessings, purpose, and lessons this day holds.

## Evening Gratitude

Father, thank You for the beauty, blessings, purpose, and lessons You revealed today.

_____

_____

_____

_____

_____

_____

_____

_____

The Seasons Journal

**Date:** _____

### Morning Declaration & Prayer

Today, I will *lean into* the things God has called me to give my heart and focus to.
I will *listen and obey* God's voice.
I will *trust His plan* and *lay down* the things I'm not called to carry in this season.
I will *lift in prayer* the people, situations, and dreams God has entrusted to me.
I will remain *teachable* and embrace the lessons today brings.

**Prayer:** Father, open my eyes and heart to perceive things from Heaven's perspective and to recognize the beauty, blessings, purpose, and lessons this day holds.

### Evening Gratitude

Father, thank You for the beauty, blessings, purpose, and lessons You revealed today.

_____

_____

_____

_____

_____

_____

_____

_____

The Seasons Journal

**Date:** _____

### Morning Declaration & Prayer

Today, I will *lean into* the things God has called me to give my heart and focus to.

I will *listen and obey* God's voice.

I will *trust His plan* and *lay down* the things I'm not called to carry in this season.

I will *lift in prayer* the people, situations, and dreams God has entrusted to me.

I will remain *teachable* and embrace the lessons today brings.

**Prayer:** Father, open my eyes and heart to perceive things from Heaven's perspective and to recognize the beauty, blessings, purpose, and lessons this day holds.

### Evening Gratitude

Father, thank You for the beauty, blessings, purpose, and lessons You revealed today.

_____

_____

_____

_____

_____

_____

_____

_____

The Seasons Journal

**Date:** _____

### Morning Declaration & Prayer

Today, I will *lean into* the things God has called me to give my heart and focus to.
I will *listen and obey* God's voice.
I will *trust His plan* and *lay down* the things I'm not called to carry in this season.
I will *lift in prayer* the people, situations, and dreams God has entrusted to me.
I will remain *teachable* and embrace the lessons today brings.

**Prayer:** Father, open my eyes and heart to perceive things from Heaven's perspective and to recognize the beauty, blessings, purpose, and lessons this day holds.

### Evening Gratitude

Father, thank You for the beauty, blessings, purpose, and lessons You revealed today.

_____

_____

_____

_____

_____

_____

_____

_____

The Seasons Journal

**Date:** _____

### Morning Declaration & Prayer

Today, I will *lean into* the things God has called me to give my heart and focus to.
I will *listen and obey* God's voice.
I will *trust His plan* and *lay down* the things I'm not called to carry in this season.
I will *lift in prayer* the people, situations, and dreams God has entrusted to me.
I will remain *teachable* and embrace the lessons today brings.

**Prayer:** Father, open my eyes and heart to perceive things from Heaven's perspective and to recognize the beauty, blessings, purpose, and lessons this day holds.

### Evening Gratitude

Father, thank You for the beauty, blessings, purpose, and lessons You revealed today.

_____

_____

_____

_____

_____

_____

_____

_____

The Seasons Journal

**Date:** _____

### Morning Declaration & Prayer
Today, I will *lean into* the things God has called me to give my heart and focus to.
I will *listen and obey* God's voice.
I will *trust His plan* and *lay down* the things I'm not called to carry in this season.
I will *lift in prayer* the people, situations, and dreams God has entrusted to me.
I will remain *teachable* and embrace the lessons today brings.

**Prayer:** Father, open my eyes and heart to perceive things from Heaven's perspective and to recognize the beauty, blessings, purpose, and lessons this day holds.

### Evening Gratitude
Father, thank You for the beauty, blessings, purpose, and lessons You revealed today.

_____

_____

_____

_____

_____

_____

_____

_____

The Seasons Journal

**Date:** _____

### Morning Declaration & Prayer

Today, I will *lean into* the things God has called me to give my heart and focus to.
I will *listen and obey* God's voice.
I will *trust His plan* and *lay down* the things I'm not called to carry in this season.
I will *lift in prayer* the people, situations, and dreams God has entrusted to me.
I will remain *teachable* and embrace the lessons today brings.

**Prayer:** Father, open my eyes and heart to perceive things from Heaven's perspective and to recognize the beauty, blessings, purpose, and lessons this day holds.

### Evening Gratitude

Father, thank You for the beauty, blessings, purpose, and lessons You revealed today.

_____

_____

_____

_____

_____

_____

_____

_____

The Seasons Journal

**Date:** _____

### Morning Declaration & Prayer

Today, I will *lean into* the things God has called me to give my heart and focus to.
I will *listen and obey* God's voice.
I will *trust His plan* and *lay down* the things I'm not called to carry in this season.
I will *lift in prayer* the people, situations, and dreams God has entrusted to me.
I will remain *teachable* and embrace the lessons today brings.

**Prayer:** Father, open my eyes and heart to perceive things from Heaven's perspective and to recognize the beauty, blessings, purpose, and lessons this day holds.

### Evening Gratitude

Father, thank You for the beauty, blessings, purpose, and lessons You revealed today.

_____

_____

_____

_____

_____

_____

_____

_____

The Seasons Journal

**Date:** _____

### Morning Declaration & Prayer

Today, I will *lean into* the things God has called me to give my heart and focus to.
I will *listen and obey* God's voice.
I will *trust His plan* and *lay down* the things I'm not called to carry in this season.
I will *lift in prayer* the people, situations, and dreams God has entrusted to me.
I will remain *teachable* and embrace the lessons today brings.

**Prayer:** Father, open my eyes and heart to perceive things from Heaven's perspective and to recognize the beauty, blessings, purpose, and lessons this day holds.

### Evening Gratitude

Father, thank You for the beauty, blessings, purpose, and lessons You revealed today.

_____

_____

_____

_____

_____

_____

_____

_____

The Seasons Journal

**Date:** _____

### Morning Declaration & Prayer

Today, I will *lean into* the things God has called me to give my heart and focus to.
I will *listen and obey* God's voice.
I will *trust His plan* and *lay down* the things I'm not called to carry in this season.
I will *lift in prayer* the people, situations, and dreams God has entrusted to me.
I will remain *teachable* and embrace the lessons today brings.

**Prayer:** Father, open my eyes and heart to perceive things from Heaven's perspective and to recognize the beauty, blessings, purpose, and lessons this day holds.

### Evening Gratitude

Father, thank You for the beauty, blessings, purpose, and lessons You revealed today.

_____

_____

_____

_____

_____

_____

_____

_____

The Seasons Journal

**Date:** _____

### Morning Declaration & Prayer

Today, I will *lean into* the things God has called me to give my heart and focus to.
I will *listen and obey* God's voice.
I will *trust His plan* and *lay down* the things I'm not called to carry in this season.
I will *lift in prayer* the people, situations, and dreams God has entrusted to me.
I will remain *teachable* and embrace the lessons today brings.

**Prayer:** Father, open my eyes and heart to perceive things from Heaven's perspective and to recognize the beauty, blessings, purpose, and lessons this day holds.

### Evening Gratitude

Father, thank You for the beauty, blessings, purpose, and lessons You revealed today.

_____

_____

_____

_____

_____

_____

_____

_____

_____

The Seasons Journal

**Date:** _____

### Morning Declaration & Prayer

Today, I will *lean into* the things God has called me to give my heart and focus to.
I will *listen and obey* God's voice.
I will *trust His plan* and *lay down* the things I'm not called to carry in this season.
I will *lift in prayer* the people, situations, and dreams God has entrusted to me.
I will remain *teachable* and embrace the lessons today brings.

**Prayer:** Father, open my eyes and heart to perceive things from Heaven's perspective and to recognize the beauty, blessings, purpose, and lessons this day holds.

### Evening Gratitude

Father, thank You for the beauty, blessings, purpose, and lessons You revealed today.

_____

_____

_____

_____

_____

_____

_____

_____

The Seasons Journal

**Date:** _____

### Morning Declaration & Prayer

Today, I will *lean into* the things God has called me to give my heart and focus to.
I will *listen and obey* God's voice.
I will *trust His plan* and *lay down* the things I'm not called to carry in this season.
I will *lift in prayer* the people, situations, and dreams God has entrusted to me.
I will remain *teachable* and embrace the lessons today brings.

**Prayer:** Father, open my eyes and heart to perceive things from Heaven's perspective and to recognize the beauty, blessings, purpose, and lessons this day holds.

### Evening Gratitude

Father, thank You for the beauty, blessings, purpose, and lessons You revealed today.

_____

_____

_____

_____

_____

_____

_____

_____

The Seasons Journal

**Date:** _____

## Morning Declaration & Prayer

Today, I will *lean into* the things God has called me to give my heart and focus to.
I will *listen and obey* God's voice.
I will *trust His plan* and *lay down* the things I'm not called to carry in this season.
I will *lift in prayer* the people, situations, and dreams God has entrusted to me.
I will remain *teachable* and embrace the lessons today brings.

**Prayer:** Father, open my eyes and heart to perceive things from Heaven's perspective and to recognize the beauty, blessings, purpose, and lessons this day holds.

## Evening Gratitude

Father, thank You for the beauty, blessings, purpose, and lessons You revealed today.

_____

_____

_____

_____

_____

_____

_____

_____

The Seasons Journal

**Date:** _____

### Morning Declaration & Prayer

Today, I will *lean into* the things God has called me to give my heart and focus to.

I will *listen and obey* God's voice.

I will *trust His plan* and *lay down* the things I'm not called to carry in this season.

I will *lift in prayer* the people, situations, and dreams God has entrusted to me.

I will remain *teachable* and embrace the lessons today brings.

**Prayer:** Father, open my eyes and heart to perceive things from Heaven's perspective and to recognize the beauty, blessings, purpose, and lessons this day holds.

### Evening Gratitude

Father, thank You for the beauty, blessings, purpose, and lessons You revealed today.

_____

_____

_____

_____

_____

_____

_____

_____

The Seasons Journal

**Date:** _____

### Morning Declaration & Prayer

Today, I will *lean into* the things God has called me to give my heart and focus to.
I will *listen and obey* God's voice.
I will *trust His plan* and *lay down* the things I'm not called to carry in this season.
I will *lift in prayer* the people, situations, and dreams God has entrusted to me.
I will remain *teachable* and embrace the lessons today brings.

**Prayer:** Father, open my eyes and heart to perceive things from Heaven's perspective and to recognize the beauty, blessings, purpose, and lessons this day holds.

### Evening Gratitude

Father, thank You for the beauty, blessings, purpose, and lessons You revealed today.

_____

_____

_____

_____

_____

_____

_____

_____

The Seasons Journal

**Date:** _____

### Morning Declaration & Prayer

Today, I will *lean into* the things God has called me to give my heart and focus to.
I will *listen and obey* God's voice.
I will *trust His plan* and *lay down* the things I'm not called to carry in this season.
I will *lift in prayer* the people, situations, and dreams God has entrusted to me.
I will remain *teachable* and embrace the lessons today brings.

**Prayer:** Father, open my eyes and heart to perceive things from Heaven's perspective and to recognize the beauty, blessings, purpose, and lessons this day holds.

### Evening Gratitude

Father, thank You for the beauty, blessings, purpose, and lessons You revealed today.

_____
_____
_____
_____
_____
_____
_____
_____
_____

The Seasons Journal

**Date:** _____

### Morning Declaration & Prayer
Today, I will *lean into* the things God has called me to give my heart and focus to.
I will *listen and obey* God's voice.
I will *trust His plan* and *lay down* the things I'm not called to carry in this season.
I will *lift in prayer* the people, situations, and dreams God has entrusted to me.
I will remain *teachable* and embrace the lessons today brings.

**Prayer:** Father, open my eyes and heart to perceive things from Heaven's perspective and to recognize the beauty, blessings, purpose, and lessons this day holds.

### Evening Gratitude
Father, thank You for the beauty, blessings, purpose, and lessons You revealed today.

_____

_____

_____

_____

_____

_____

_____

_____

The Seasons Journal

**Date:** _____

### Morning Declaration & Prayer

Today, I will *lean into* the things God has called me to give my heart and focus to.
I will *listen and obey* God's voice.
I will *trust His plan* and *lay down* the things I'm not called to carry in this season.
I will *lift in prayer* the people, situations, and dreams God has entrusted to me.
I will remain *teachable* and embrace the lessons today brings.

**Prayer:** Father, open my eyes and heart to perceive things from Heaven's perspective and to recognize the beauty, blessings, purpose, and lessons this day holds.

### Evening Gratitude

Father, thank You for the beauty, blessings, purpose, and lessons You revealed today.

_____

_____

_____

_____

_____

_____

_____

_____

The Seasons Journal

**Date:** _____

### Morning Declaration & Prayer

Today, I will *lean into* the things God has called me to give my heart and focus to.
I will *listen and obey* God's voice.
I will *trust His plan* and *lay down* the things I'm not called to carry in this season.
I will *lift in prayer* the people, situations, and dreams God has entrusted to me.
I will remain *teachable* and embrace the lessons today brings.

**Prayer:** Father, open my eyes and heart to perceive things from Heaven's perspective and to recognize the beauty, blessings, purpose, and lessons this day holds.

### Evening Gratitude

Father, thank You for the beauty, blessings, purpose, and lessons You revealed today.

_____

_____

_____

_____

_____

_____

_____

_____

_____

The Seasons Journal

**Date:** _____

### Morning Declaration & Prayer

Today, I will *lean into* the things God has called me to give my heart and focus to.
I will *listen and obey* God's voice.
I will *trust His plan* and *lay down* the things I'm not called to carry in this season.
I will *lift in prayer* the people, situations, and dreams God has entrusted to me.
I will remain *teachable* and embrace the lessons today brings.

**Prayer:** Father, open my eyes and heart to perceive things from Heaven's perspective and to recognize the beauty, blessings, purpose, and lessons this day holds.

### Evening Gratitude

Father, thank You for the beauty, blessings, purpose, and lessons You revealed today.

_____

_____

_____

_____

_____

_____

_____

_____

_____

The Seasons Journal

**Date:** _____

### Morning Declaration & Prayer

Today, I will *lean into* the things God has called me to give my heart and focus to.
I will *listen and obey* God's voice.
I will *trust His plan* and *lay down* the things I'm not called to carry in this season.
I will *lift in prayer* the people, situations, and dreams God has entrusted to me.
I will remain *teachable* and embrace the lessons today brings.

**Prayer:** Father, open my eyes and heart to perceive things from Heaven's perspective and to recognize the beauty, blessings, purpose, and lessons this day holds.

### Evening Gratitude

Father, thank You for the beauty, blessings, purpose, and lessons You revealed today.

_____

_____

_____

_____

_____

_____

_____

_____

The Seasons Journal

**Date:** _____

## Morning Declaration & Prayer

Today, I will *lean into* the things God has called me to give my heart and focus to.
I will *listen and obey* God's voice.
I will *trust His plan* and *lay down* the things I'm not called to carry in this season.
I will *lift in prayer* the people, situations, and dreams God has entrusted to me.
I will remain *teachable* and embrace the lessons today brings.

**Prayer:** Father, open my eyes and heart to perceive things from Heaven's perspective and to recognize the beauty, blessings, purpose, and lessons this day holds.

## Evening Gratitude

Father, thank You for the beauty, blessings, purpose, and lessons You revealed today.

_____

_____

_____

_____

_____

_____

_____

_____

_____

The Seasons Journal

**Date:** _____

### Morning Declaration & Prayer
Today, I will *lean into* the things God has called me to give my heart and focus to.
I will *listen and obey* God's voice.
I will *trust His plan* and *lay down* the things I'm not called to carry in this season.
I will *lift in prayer* the people, situations, and dreams God has entrusted to me.
I will remain *teachable* and embrace the lessons today brings.

**Prayer:** Father, open my eyes and heart to perceive things from Heaven's perspective and to recognize the beauty, blessings, purpose, and lessons this day holds.

### Evening Gratitude
Father, thank You for the beauty, blessings, purpose, and lessons You revealed today.

_____

_____

_____

_____

_____

_____

_____

_____

_____

The Seasons Journal

**Date:** _____

### Morning Declaration & Prayer

Today, I will *lean into* the things God has called me to give my heart and focus to.
I will *listen and obey* God's voice.
I will *trust His plan* and *lay down* the things I'm not called to carry in this season.
I will *lift in prayer* the people, situations, and dreams God has entrusted to me.
I will remain *teachable* and embrace the lessons today brings.

**Prayer:** Father, open my eyes and heart to perceive things from Heaven's perspective and to recognize the beauty, blessings, purpose, and lessons this day holds.

### Evening Gratitude

Father, thank You for the beauty, blessings, purpose, and lessons You revealed today.

_____

_____

_____

_____

_____

_____

_____

_____

The Seasons Journal

**Date:** _____

### Morning Declaration & Prayer

Today, I will *lean into* the things God has called me to give my heart and focus to.
I will *listen and obey* God's voice.
I will *trust His plan* and *lay down* the things I'm not called to carry in this season.
I will *lift in prayer* the people, situations, and dreams God has entrusted to me.
I will remain *teachable* and embrace the lessons today brings.

**Prayer:** Father, open my eyes and heart to perceive things from Heaven's perspective and to recognize the beauty, blessings, purpose, and lessons this day holds.

### Evening Gratitude

Father, thank You for the beauty, blessings, purpose, and lessons You revealed today.

_____

_____

_____

_____

_____

_____

_____

_____

The Seasons Journal

**Date:** _____

## Morning Declaration & Prayer

Today, I will *lean into* the things God has called me to give my heart and focus to.
I will *listen and obey* God's voice.
I will *trust His plan* and *lay down* the things I'm not called to carry in this season.
I will *lift in prayer* the people, situations, and dreams God has entrusted to me.
I will remain *teachable* and embrace the lessons today brings.

**Prayer:** Father, open my eyes and heart to perceive things from Heaven's perspective and to recognize the beauty, blessings, purpose, and lessons this day holds.

## Evening Gratitude

Father, thank You for the beauty, blessings, purpose, and lessons You revealed today.

_____

_____

_____

_____

_____

_____

_____

_____

The Seasons Journal

**Date:** _____

### Morning Declaration & Prayer

Today, I will *lean into* the things God has called me to give my heart and focus to.
I will *listen and obey* God's voice.
I will *trust His plan* and *lay down* the things I'm not called to carry in this season.
I will *lift in prayer* the people, situations, and dreams God has entrusted to me.
I will remain *teachable* and embrace the lessons today brings.

**Prayer:** Father, open my eyes and heart to perceive things from Heaven's perspective and to recognize the beauty, blessings, purpose, and lessons this day holds.

### Evening Gratitude

Father, thank You for the beauty, blessings, purpose, and lessons You revealed today.

_____

_____

_____

_____

_____

_____

_____

_____

The Seasons Journal

**Date:** _____

### Morning Declaration & Prayer

Today, I will *lean into* the things God has called me to give my heart and focus to.
I will *listen and obey* God's voice.
I will *trust His plan* and *lay down* the things I'm not called to carry in this season.
I will *lift in prayer* the people, situations, and dreams God has entrusted to me.
I will remain *teachable* and embrace the lessons today brings.

**Prayer:** Father, open my eyes and heart to perceive things from Heaven's perspective and to recognize the beauty, blessings, purpose, and lessons this day holds.

### Evening Gratitude

Father, thank You for the beauty, blessings, purpose, and lessons You revealed today.

_____

_____

_____

_____

_____

_____

_____

_____

_____

The Seasons Journal

**Date:** _____

### Morning Declaration & Prayer
Today, I will *lean into* the things God has called me to give my heart and focus to.
I will *listen and obey* God's voice.
I will *trust His plan* and *lay down* the things I'm not called to carry in this season.
I will *lift in prayer* the people, situations, and dreams God has entrusted to me.
I will remain *teachable* and embrace the lessons today brings.

**Prayer:** Father, open my eyes and heart to perceive things from Heaven's perspective and to recognize the beauty, blessings, purpose, and lessons this day holds.

### Evening Gratitude
Father, thank You for the beauty, blessings, purpose, and lessons You revealed today.

_____

_____

_____

_____

_____

_____

_____

_____

_____

The Seasons Journal

**Date:** _____

### Morning Declaration & Prayer

Today, I will *lean into* the things God has called me to give my heart and focus to.
I will *listen and obey* God's voice.
I will *trust His plan* and *lay down* the things I'm not called to carry in this season.
I will *lift in prayer* the people, situations, and dreams God has entrusted to me.
I will remain *teachable* and embrace the lessons today brings.

**Prayer:** Father, open my eyes and heart to perceive things from Heaven's perspective and to recognize the beauty, blessings, purpose, and lessons this day holds.

### Evening Gratitude

Father, thank You for the beauty, blessings, purpose, and lessons You revealed today.

_____

_____

_____

_____

_____

_____

_____

_____

The Seasons Journal

**Date:** _____

### Morning Declaration & Prayer

Today, I will *lean into* the things God has called me to give my heart and focus to.
I will *listen and obey* God's voice.
I will *trust His plan* and *lay down* the things I'm not called to carry in this season.
I will *lift in prayer* the people, situations, and dreams God has entrusted to me.
I will remain *teachable* and embrace the lessons today brings.

**Prayer:** Father, open my eyes and heart to perceive things from Heaven's perspective and to recognize the beauty, blessings, purpose, and lessons this day holds.

### Evening Gratitude

Father, thank You for the beauty, blessings, purpose, and lessons You revealed today.

_____
_____
_____
_____
_____
_____
_____
_____
_____

The Seasons Journal

**Date:** _____

### Morning Declaration & Prayer
Today, I will *lean into* the things God has called me to give my heart and focus to.
I will *listen and obey* God's voice.
I will *trust His plan* and *lay down* the things I'm not called to carry in this season.
I will *lift in prayer* the people, situations, and dreams God has entrusted to me.
I will remain *teachable* and embrace the lessons today brings.

**Prayer:** Father, open my eyes and heart to perceive things from Heaven's perspective and to recognize the beauty, blessings, purpose, and lessons this day holds.

### Evening Gratitude
Father, thank You for the beauty, blessings, purpose, and lessons You revealed today.

_____

_____

_____

_____

_____

_____

_____

_____

The Seasons Journal

**Date:** _____

### Morning Declaration & Prayer

Today, I will *lean into* the things God has called me to give my heart and focus to.
I will *listen and obey* God's voice.
I will *trust His plan* and *lay down* the things I'm not called to carry in this season.
I will *lift in prayer* the people, situations, and dreams God has entrusted to me.
I will remain *teachable* and embrace the lessons today brings.

**Prayer:** Father, open my eyes and heart to perceive things from Heaven's perspective and to recognize the beauty, blessings, purpose, and lessons this day holds.

### Evening Gratitude

Father, thank You for the beauty, blessings, purpose, and lessons You revealed today.

_____

_____

_____

_____

_____

_____

_____

_____

The Seasons Journal

**Date:** _____

## Morning Declaration & Prayer

Today, I will *lean into* the things God has called me to give my heart and focus to.
I will *listen and obey* God's voice.
I will *trust His plan* and *lay down* the things I'm not called to carry in this season.
I will *lift in prayer* the people, situations, and dreams God has entrusted to me.
I will remain *teachable* and embrace the lessons today brings.

**Prayer:** Father, open my eyes and heart to perceive things from Heaven's perspective and to recognize the beauty, blessings, purpose, and lessons this day holds.

## Evening Gratitude

Father, thank You for the beauty, blessings, purpose, and lessons You revealed today.

_____
_____
_____
_____
_____
_____
_____
_____

The Seasons Journal

**Date:** _____

### Morning Declaration & Prayer

Today, I will *lean into* the things God has called me to give my heart and focus to.
I will *listen and obey* God's voice.
I will *trust His plan* and *lay down* the things I'm not called to carry in this season.
I will *lift in prayer* the people, situations, and dreams God has entrusted to me.
I will remain *teachable* and embrace the lessons today brings.

**Prayer:** Father, open my eyes and heart to perceive things from Heaven's perspective and to recognize the beauty, blessings, purpose, and lessons this day holds.

### Evening Gratitude

Father, thank You for the beauty, blessings, purpose, and lessons You revealed today.

_____

_____

_____

_____

_____

_____

_____

_____

_____

The Seasons Journal

**Date:** _____

### Morning Declaration & Prayer

Today, I will *lean into* the things God has called me to give my heart and focus to.
I will *listen and obey* God's voice.
I will *trust His plan* and *lay down* the things I'm not called to carry in this season.
I will *lift in prayer* the people, situations, and dreams God has entrusted to me.
I will remain *teachable* and embrace the lessons today brings.

**Prayer:** Father, open my eyes and heart to perceive things from Heaven's perspective and to recognize the beauty, blessings, purpose, and lessons this day holds.

### Evening Gratitude

Father, thank You for the beauty, blessings, purpose, and lessons You revealed today.

_____

_____

_____

_____

_____

_____

_____

_____

_____

The Seasons Journal

**Date:** _____

### Morning Declaration & Prayer

Today, I will *lean into* the things God has called me to give my heart and focus to.
I will *listen and obey* God's voice.
I will *trust His plan* and *lay down* the things I'm not called to carry in this season.
I will *lift in prayer* the people, situations, and dreams God has entrusted to me.
I will remain *teachable* and embrace the lessons today brings.

**Prayer:** Father, open my eyes and heart to perceive things from Heaven's perspective and to recognize the beauty, blessings, purpose, and lessons this day holds.

### Evening Gratitude

Father, thank You for the beauty, blessings, purpose, and lessons You revealed today.

_____

_____

_____

_____

_____

_____

_____

_____

The Seasons Journal

**Date:** _____

### Morning Declaration & Prayer

Today, I will *lean into* the things God has called me to give my heart and focus to.
I will *listen and obey* God's voice.
I will *trust His plan* and *lay down* the things I'm not called to carry in this season.
I will *lift in prayer* the people, situations, and dreams God has entrusted to me.
I will remain *teachable* and embrace the lessons today brings.

**Prayer:** Father, open my eyes and heart to perceive things from Heaven's perspective and to recognize the beauty, blessings, purpose, and lessons this day holds.

### Evening Gratitude

Father, thank You for the beauty, blessings, purpose, and lessons You revealed today.

_____

_____

_____

_____

_____

_____

_____

_____

The Seasons Journal

**Date:** _____

### Morning Declaration & Prayer

Today, I will *lean into* the things God has called me to give my heart and focus to.
I will *listen and obey* God's voice.
I will *trust His plan* and *lay down* the things I'm not called to carry in this season.
I will *lift in prayer* the people, situations, and dreams God has entrusted to me.
I will remain *teachable* and embrace the lessons today brings.

**Prayer:** Father, open my eyes and heart to perceive things from Heaven's perspective and to recognize the beauty, blessings, purpose, and lessons this day holds.

### Evening Gratitude

Father, thank You for the beauty, blessings, purpose, and lessons You revealed today.

_____

_____

_____

_____

_____

_____

_____

_____

The Seasons Journal

**Date:** _____

## Morning Declaration & Prayer

Today, I will *lean into* the things God has called me to give my heart and focus to.
I will *listen and obey* God's voice.
I will *trust His plan* and *lay down* the things I'm not called to carry in this season.
I will *lift in prayer* the people, situations, and dreams God has entrusted to me.
I will remain *teachable* and embrace the lessons today brings.

**Prayer:** Father, open my eyes and heart to perceive things from Heaven's perspective and to recognize the beauty, blessings, purpose, and lessons this day holds.

## Evening Gratitude

Father, thank You for the beauty, blessings, purpose, and lessons You revealed today.

_____

_____

_____

_____

_____

_____

_____

_____

_____

The Seasons Journal

**Date:** _____

### Morning Declaration & Prayer
Today, I will *lean into* the things God has called me to give my heart and focus to.
I will *listen and obey* God's voice.
I will *trust His plan* and *lay down* the things I'm not called to carry in this season.
I will *lift in prayer* the people, situations, and dreams God has entrusted to me.
I will remain *teachable* and embrace the lessons today brings.

**Prayer:** Father, open my eyes and heart to perceive things from Heaven's perspective and to recognize the beauty, blessings, purpose, and lessons this day holds.

### Evening Gratitude
Father, thank You for the beauty, blessings, purpose, and lessons You revealed today.

_____

_____

_____

_____

_____

_____

_____

_____

_____

The Seasons Journal

**Date:** _____

### Morning Declaration & Prayer

Today, I will *lean into* the things God has called me to give my heart and focus to.
I will *listen and obey* God's voice.
I will *trust His plan* and *lay down* the things I'm not called to carry in this season.
I will *lift in prayer* the people, situations, and dreams God has entrusted to me.
I will remain *teachable* and embrace the lessons today brings.

**Prayer:** Father, open my eyes and heart to perceive things from Heaven's perspective and to recognize the beauty, blessings, purpose, and lessons this day holds.

### Evening Gratitude

Father, thank You for the beauty, blessings, purpose, and lessons You revealed today.

_____

_____

_____

_____

_____

_____

_____

_____

The Seasons Journal

**Date:** _____

### Morning Declaration & Prayer

Today, I will *lean into* the things God has called me to give my heart and focus to.
I will *listen and obey* God's voice.
I will *trust His plan* and *lay down* the things I'm not called to carry in this season.
I will *lift in prayer* the people, situations, and dreams God has entrusted to me.
I will remain *teachable* and embrace the lessons today brings.

**Prayer:** Father, open my eyes and heart to perceive things from Heaven's perspective and to recognize the beauty, blessings, purpose, and lessons this day holds.

### Evening Gratitude

Father, thank You for the beauty, blessings, purpose, and lessons You revealed today.

_____

_____

_____

_____

_____

_____

_____

_____

The Seasons Journal

**Date:** _____

## Morning Declaration & Prayer

Today, I will *lean into* the things God has called me to give my heart and focus to.

I will *listen and obey* God's voice.

I will *trust His plan* and *lay down* the things I'm not called to carry in this season.

I will *lift in prayer* the people, situations, and dreams God has entrusted to me.

I will remain *teachable* and embrace the lessons today brings.

**Prayer:** Father, open my eyes and heart to perceive things from Heaven's perspective and to recognize the beauty, blessings, purpose, and lessons this day holds.

## Evening Gratitude

Father, thank You for the beauty, blessings, purpose, and lessons You revealed today.

_____

_____

_____

_____

_____

_____

_____

_____

_____

The Seasons Journal

**Date:** _____

### Morning Declaration & Prayer

Today, I will *lean into* the things God has called me to give my heart and focus to.
I will *listen and obey* God's voice.
I will *trust His plan* and *lay down* the things I'm not called to carry in this season.
I will *lift in prayer* the people, situations, and dreams God has entrusted to me.
I will remain *teachable* and embrace the lessons today brings.

**Prayer:** Father, open my eyes and heart to perceive things from Heaven's perspective and to recognize the beauty, blessings, purpose, and lessons this day holds.

### Evening Gratitude

Father, thank You for the beauty, blessings, purpose, and lessons You revealed today.

_____

_____

_____

_____

_____

_____

_____

_____

The Seasons Journal

**Date:** _____

### Morning Declaration & Prayer
Today, I will *lean into* the things God has called me to give my heart and focus to.
I will *listen and obey* God's voice.
I will *trust His plan* and *lay down* the things I'm not called to carry in this season.
I will *lift in prayer* the people, situations, and dreams God has entrusted to me.
I will remain *teachable* and embrace the lessons today brings.

**Prayer:** Father, open my eyes and heart to perceive things from Heaven's perspective and to recognize the beauty, blessings, purpose, and lessons this day holds.

### Evening Gratitude
Father, thank You for the beauty, blessings, purpose, and lessons You revealed today.

_____

_____

_____

_____

_____

_____

_____

_____

_____

_____

The Seasons Journal

**Date:** _____


### Morning Declaration & Prayer
Today, I will *lean into* the things God has called me to give my heart and focus to.
I will *listen and obey* God's voice.
I will *trust His plan* and *lay down* the things I'm not called to carry in this season.
I will *lift in prayer* the people, situations, and dreams God has entrusted to me.
I will remain *teachable* and embrace the lessons today brings.


**Prayer:** Father, open my eyes and heart to perceive things from Heaven's perspective and to recognize the beauty, blessings, purpose, and lessons this day holds.


### Evening Gratitude
Father, thank You for the beauty, blessings, purpose, and lessons You revealed today.

_____

_____

_____

_____

_____

_____

_____

_____

The Seasons Journal

**Date:** _____

### Morning Declaration & Prayer

Today, I will *lean into* the things God has called me to give my heart and focus to.
I will *listen and obey* God's voice.
I will *trust His plan* and *lay down* the things I'm not called to carry in this season.
I will *lift in prayer* the people, situations, and dreams God has entrusted to me.
I will remain *teachable* and embrace the lessons today brings.

**Prayer:** Father, open my eyes and heart to perceive things from Heaven's perspective and to recognize the beauty, blessings, purpose, and lessons this day holds.

### Evening Gratitude

Father, thank You for the beauty, blessings, purpose, and lessons You revealed today.

_____

_____

_____

_____

_____

_____

_____

_____

The Seasons Journal

**Date:** _____

### Morning Declaration & Prayer

Today, I will *lean into* the things God has called me to give my heart and focus to.
I will *listen and obey* God's voice.
I will *trust His plan* and *lay down* the things I'm not called to carry in this season.
I will *lift in prayer* the people, situations, and dreams God has entrusted to me.
I will remain *teachable* and embrace the lessons today brings.

**Prayer:** Father, open my eyes and heart to perceive things from Heaven's perspective and to recognize the beauty, blessings, purpose, and lessons this day holds.

### Evening Gratitude

Father, thank You for the beauty, blessings, purpose, and lessons You revealed today.

_____

_____

_____

_____

_____

_____

_____

_____

The Seasons Journal

**Date:** _____

### Morning Declaration & Prayer

Today, I will *lean into* the things God has called me to give my heart and focus to.
I will *listen and obey* God's voice.
I will *trust His plan* and *lay down* the things I'm not called to carry in this season.
I will *lift in prayer* the people, situations, and dreams God has entrusted to me.
I will remain *teachable* and embrace the lessons today brings.

**Prayer:** Father, open my eyes and heart to perceive things from Heaven's perspective and to recognize the beauty, blessings, purpose, and lessons this day holds.

### Evening Gratitude

Father, thank You for the beauty, blessings, purpose, and lessons You revealed today.

_____

_____

_____

_____

_____

_____

_____

_____

_____

The Seasons Journal

# Season Reflections

Look back with gratitude before stepping into what's next.

**As one season ends and another begins, take time to pause and reflect on what God has done.**
This is your opportunity to look back with gratitude, recognize His faithfulness, and gather the beauty, blessings, purpose, and lessons you've received before stepping into your next season.

- How was God's beauty and blessings revealed in this season?
- In what ways was God's purpose for this season made clear?
- Did I remain focused on what God called me to give my heart and attention to?
- How did I learn to discern God's voice more clearly in my daily life?
- What key lessons will I carry forward into my next season?

**Prayer:** *Father, thank You for walking with me through this season. Thank You for the beauty and blessings You revealed, the purpose You made known, and the lessons You taught along the way. As I prepare to step into the next season, help me carry forward the wisdom, faith, and grace You've cultivated in me. May I continue to see every season as part of Your unfolding plan for my life.*

**A Blessing for Your Next Season:** *May you walk in step with God through every season of your life. May His beauty surround you, His blessings overflow, His purpose sustain you, and His lessons shape you. And may your heart remain open to the new things He is doing—trusting that in every ending, a new beginning is already unfolding in His perfect time.*

_____

_____

_____

# The Seasons Journal

# The Seasons Journal

The Seasons Journal

# Discover Other Books & Resources

## by Krista Pettiford
### kristapettiford.com

**Books**
• *A Call to God's Daughters: Step Into His L.A.B. — Love, Acceptance, and Beauty* (Based on the Book of Ruth)
• *Called Out: Walking in Your Calling with Clarity, Confidence, and Courage*
• *Surrendered Balance: Daily Living for God's Daughters*

**YouVersion Devotionals**
• *Brave Change — Navigating Unexpected Seasons*
• *Embracing the Fullness of Your Calling in Christ*
• *Holding Onto Hope in Your Waiting Season*

The Seasons Journal

www.ingramcontent.com/pod-product-compliance
Lightning Source LLC
Chambersburg PA
CBHW020244010526
44107CB00002B/91